THE CULT *of* SEIZURE

THE CULT *of* SEIZURE

&

THE DEEP ZOO
Two Essays

RIKKI DUCORNET

SKYLIGHT PRESS

This edition published in Great Britain in 2012 by Skylight Press, 210 Brooklyn Road, Cheltenham, Glos GL51 8EA

The Cult of Seizure was first published in Canada in 1989 by The Porcupine's Quill Inc, Erin, Ontario.

The Deep Zoo: Two Essays was first published in the USA in 2004 by Obscure Publications, Black River Falls, Wisconsin.

Cover artwork by Rikki Ducornet
Designed and typeset by Rebsie Fairholm
Publisher: Daniel Staniforth

www.skylightpress.co.uk

Printed and bound in Great Britain by Lightning Source, Milton Keynes. Typeset in Mrs Eaves 13/16pt, a font by Zuzana Licko.

British Library Cataloguing in Publication Data.
A catalogue record for this book is available from the British Library.

ISBN 978-1-908011-46-6

And the eye of the devil upon us
Closing drunkenly in from all sides ...
— James Dickey, *Helmets*

I. MONKEYWIND

Erzsébet Báthory, the 'Bloody Countess', was born
in Hungary in 1560 and died in 1614, walled into
her bed-chamber in the castle at Csejthe by order of
the King. By the time she was brought to trial by her
cousin Thurzó, she and her servants – the hag Jó Ilona
and the gnome Ficzkó – had murdered over 600 young
women.

Between seizures, Erzsébet spent her time gazing at
her reflection in a mirror. Her deadly narcissism was
rooted in an overwhelming dread of decay. Her hags
assured her that baths of fresh blood would keep her
young; murder was her strategy for survival.

Her last victim, the fair Doricza, was discovered by
Thurzó flayed alive the morning after the feast of
Christmas.

PROLOGUE

Havoc accelerates
And Time a sigh
Blowing through a hollow bone.
In the sky, the zodiac impaled
Petrifies.

This is not a celebration.
It is the sound the door makes when
The monkeywind of seizure
Shuts us in.

O | A WHEEL OF EELS

She slides from the womb
dragging cyclones, thumb-screws and sparks.
She snuggles beneath the caul with a rattlesnake
and snarling, barks.

The midwife sees the stellar eel
traced upon the infant's skull.
The thirteen puncture marks are peculiar.
The knotted cord tenses to strike her.

The midwife breaks out in hives
as wasps slam against the glass.
Cloaks and daggers!
She kisses a crucifix worried by weasels.

An archon – the first of seven –
holds the smoking candle.
The turquoise flame hisses and reels.

The midwife is drowned in a sack of stones.
Her bones agitate with eels.

This house in wolftime
an island inhabited by demons.
Not he, nor she, but *it* and *it*
that like the moon shed scales
causing things to decompose.

This is not the folly of wine
but the brine of Death.
Desperate coupling
of demons come unsexed.
And hit and hit
hard in mind.
And hearts adrift
in devil-rhyme.

Infirmity circles the mountain.
In the air the wings of Grim
a clamour in the valley of Stealth.
Pin. Razor. Flame. Finger.
The clatter of butchery. Hunger.
The ugly mazes of mind and mirror.

Convulsed the countess chokes on breath
temple pierced by arrow, body by spire
and everywhere fire
and Death.

The Golem of her heart lisps: linger.

Witches hop croaking from the pyre
Gunpowder tied to their throats with wire.
Anything is possible. Anything at all!
Hypochondria! Melancholia!

Eat snow, Erzsébet; may your lips be cold –
The world is burning.
Rub your lips with snow, name the hour,
Kneel before the first man you see.
He will be horned.

Tear from the earth a rooted man;
Animated by the heat of your hand
He will struggle and try to bite.
Threaten him with fire. Lick him with your cold tongue.
He will relent, foretell the moves of constellations
And instruct in the secrets of pleasure.

He will sing of the girl crushed beneath the moon,
Of the sting of the King's scorpion,
The exact words of the talking Teraphim;
Together you will dismember Eve.

Blue spirit, white spirit
Spirit of the knife –
You will hold him to your lips.
You will play the Game of Breathings.

Endings.

To be tossed to the eye of the storm;
Trance is the colour of Lucifer's horn.

What is the colour of coma? White –
Inertia, the snowy tracks
Someone runs and gags. And black
The spokes of wheels.
The thunder's tongue.
The milk of squids. The alphabet of dung.

What is the colour of Eternity?
Riddles swimming in their stink
And planets ticking in their ink.

I am object
Desired thing.
I am the memory
of her sting.

Woe I feel poorly
In this eelish light.
Unsafe, I scuttle,
small as fright.

See my cup swarm.
Reflect
the morning's
collapsed lung.

Gobbets on the ogre's shelf:
Bottled owl, the genitals of snakes
Pig born with horn, elf with rake.

And I, a mistake
will be erased
Without a trace.

A was fed to mice. (A is for animals dancing.)
B was bathed in ice. (B is for binding.)
C ate a cake of poison. (Menace inhabits the centre.)
D is a dog named Damage. (The Devil is his master.)
E succumbed to Evil and wandered in the night,
F the foolish fish, lured by one small light.
G the glass, the frozen grass, the glacial winds of winter;
H the nine rivers of Hell and one floating sinner.
I am Jó Ilona's iron mirror of ink, and J the
Jar of jasper, made to work the jinx.
K the knot, the kick in the head, twelve
Liquid figures of lizards in lead.

> M the mole, I dig for more
> and more than you can give.
> If I was not dying, dear,
> it could be good to live.

Numbness, Ofall, Pain and Questions
are the Risks of Storms and Tantrums.

U is Erzsébet's unclean bed,
V her velvets, black and red. And gleaming
Wetly in the path, Thurzó sees the shards of Wrath.

XGLOMANCY.

Doricza's Youth so pink, is pale and rent
    with
        nails
            of
                Zinc.

Would you live forever, quick-witted in resplendent youth,
Drink the dew from the spoor of a one-legged crone;
Roll naked in the hay, but always roll alone.
Take an axe to the spouse of a hardened heretic,
Scrape out her brain with a spoon of lead
Abstracted from the pocket of a lunatic.
And burn the empty bone, but always burn alone.
Then will your complexion be flawless,
Will you travel the roads of the world without harm,
Will you visit its teeming cities untouched by Peril,
Ferocious Beasts, Malicious Men;
Other Accidents too numerous to name.

Once I was forever;
Smooth as sleet, the palest face.
I thought my hags were clever —
Hags for all seasons.
And I impermeable to weather.

I have nothing to confess. I am a Báthory.
Damn your eyes; I am a Jackal.
My mouth a furnace. My signature – savagery.
   I am in the wings of every crime,
   Grinning in the wound.

Give it to me! Make it last!
   I am rage. Inconceivable and Unique.
Keep it coming! I never get enough.
I am a crucible.
   I sleep in the shadow of the bitter tree.
   I descend. I descend. I descend.
   I am gravity.

Kiss my mouth. Kiss my maw.
Lick my hand. It is a claw.
I want all of her. I want all.
   I am impenitent.
   I am affliction.

Take a flame to her Jó!
Burn thorns between her legs.
Burn oiled paper.

Fever, fever; shiver, shiver –
Agony fills her like wine.
I have a thirst …
And as falling stars rake the river
I worry Beauty's corpse.
I am a jackal. Near me life is always fatal.
    It is I who has given the Universe its bad name.

I am your precious poppet,
You've seen my poison pin.
I am your thorny well,
Your ribboned manikin.
And you my secret suicide –
Necklace of lies,
My nine lives.

We witness accidents
The metamorphosis of things
Into freaked particles.

As the king's bronze dragon
Crouches upon her heart,
For mercy
She would gladly burn.

She has entertained herself
With such radical games.
No sane person indulges
In such dead reckoning.

A recurring decimal
A severed
Head bounded after
The Countess' carriage.

An innocent
Out seeking employment
Saw it and crossed himself countless times.
He may have been enchanted.

A twisted cipher cleaves
The aching sum of this mind.
No sane person indulges in distractions such as these.

Name one sane person.

Beware the beast
And goblin love.
The baited glove.

Here lies the proof: Doricza
A strapping wench once cherished
Now gore and stench fresh perished.

Fathered by feebleness
the transports of thunder and hail
born with a nail in her heart.

Tantrum is her milk
and murder her feast.
Pieces of her stick like skin
to those she meets.
She is heavy beyond belief.
Her days are shallow
Her loneliness is deep.

She never remembers her dreams and yet at dawn
her bed heaves with corpses.

When God makes rain
The Devil makes hail.
When God makes hail,
The Devil makes worse.

Iron shoes boogie in the hearth;
Beauty is stripped, bent and green.
The smoke boasts: *Bile and spleen.*

Beauty, in tangled hair,
Stands seized with fear.
Erzsébet is ecstatic –

As corpses ripen in the eaves
The cards spell:
Eternity is here.

The humpback performs a trick
With a mandrake dressed in silk.
Erzsébet bites Beauty's neck.

At midnight Beauty flees
But Erzsébet is everywhere
Disguised as sky. Her spies in every tree.

When Beauty is caught and bound
Erzsébet mews:
Freedom is a myth of the mind.

Beauty screams. In the cities
The famished cry for meat
And dreams.

As Erzsébet cuts Beauty's throat
And Death is crowned Queen –
Erzsébet lies: *There is no Evil. Only Disorder.*

13 | SHE IS A ROBBER

Erzsébet straddles my dreams –
I swear, her thighs are tigers.
She comes silent, a cold spell, a variable star.

And the night is an arsonist.
She scorches towards Christmas.
Past my nebula of crabs,
My riverbed of shards.

Where is the Sandman?
His stylet? His silk noose?
Blindfolded in my familiar pit
I hug a sack of skulls.

And the night is a robber.
She hurls her way to Black Mass
Past my bridal chamber,
Star Chamber.

The lunatic algebra
of Love.
The frenzied orbits
of Mood.
The malarial temperatures
of Wound.
Symbols of the Cult
of Seizure:
This flesh, this amulet
incised.
This hot spoor
of predators.
This zodiac savaged
in the sky.

II. VIPERWEED

Thorn Falconer
was a wheel
rotating in shadow,
a stone alphabet
too smooth to break.
A city where the past
is plundered.
A huckster and a scoundrel
a highjacker of hearts.
And the heart is a jade fountain
orbited with flowers.
Some called him Señor Turquoise
the archaeological terrorist;
he sold his stolen hatchets
his masks with semi-precious eyes
to an eccentric millionaire
of infallible connections
who kept this lawless treasure
buried in coffins.
Now I think it strange
how the things Thorn lifted –
the black axes
the deep-naveled puppets –
remained underground.
The curators of three museums
were after his skin.
However he was skilful
at keeping a loose distance.
We met in a ravine
more a rock-slide than a highway;
I approached him
with my smaller nets
and watched him move.

He walked beneath
the faulted
mirrors of the sun
more a shimmer than a man
a spontaneous
generation of fire.
As wasps bolted
in the burning air
his mouth twisted
in a grin.
Now I writhe to think of it –
how I thirsted for
his horn. And stroke.
How I
kindled, tempted and riven
lingered
in the precincts of contagion.
If they called him Señor Turquoise
they had their reason:
his thoughts were sky –
as I crossed over
to the Other Side
I saw blue ether
exulting in his eyes.
Mister, that's my heart
you're treading down.
And the heart is a hoop
a feather burning in the air.
And he a flaying wheel
tearing up the road.
His thousand snakes
the violated tombs
which rattle and hiss
behind his back.

And menace walks the core
at the centre of the day;
menace in silence
the bright saws
the hooks and eyes
of insects
menace –
for example:
the way he leans
at the crossroads
where things crash together.
The spokes of the wheel
joined at the heart
like lovers colliding
embracing blind,
like insects
back to back.
Blind as the lizards I prod
from continental drifts
and pluck like crabs
from under rocks
their shadows swift.
And the heart of a lizard
is a mirror of black glass;
a frozen moon an airless planet.
High as it leaps this moon is static.
Thorn Falconer sets his plunder down
and restores the morning's steal:
gold so hard, so bright
it lacerates my sight. He says:
See: in its mouth the jaguar
holds a seed, a word, a wheel.
I say: it is a skull
with turquoise eyes.

He smiles. A dazzlement.
And I am weightless –
the ether in a lethal chamber
with bones of sugar
dressed in paper.
Beneath the solar disc
I stand inflammable.
He laughs. He laughs each time
he speaks of risk. He says:
It is the way we live –
drugged dancers
helpless and brittle
in the jaws of the tiger
in the land of the sieve.
And biting my neck whispers:
Let me dip my hand
in your easy silver.
And his love is a flower
viperweed.
A lethal flower
a tall, blue glass
of ether.
I feel his hands
flat against my back
and with a crack
split along the seam.
As our mouths squirrel
and the world dies
I wonder why a thief's tongue
tastes of Paradise.
Broken on the wheel
of his kiss
I succumb
to the orbits of serpents
and eclipse.

Sobbing for air
beneath the scalding
lenses of the sun
I, with my love of lizards
am taken by this fever: Thorn Falconer
and would wander with him
hunted, outcast and queer.
And the heart is a wheel
rolling down a precipice
a highway on fire
littered with glass.
The world is a snake
flung into a chasm;
a hollow bone
puzzled by wasps.
I have a photograph
of the room we shared;
The Book of Flowers
lies open on the bed.
It says: *Make their hearts fearless*
that they may desire
the sweetness of Death.
And it dies hard
the illusion
that sacrifice keeps
the wheels of the world
in motion.
Still it is the world's core
on the rack.
Ball players, warriors
deep-naveled maidens –
none escape the wheel;
earthquake and orbits
the vaulting moon
the yawning flower.
And our love is this wheel and this flower.

A war of wheels. A war of flowers.
And our life, Thorn says, is a seizure.
And love is a wild hare leaping
it circles until brought down.
The eye of the hunter upon us
and his eye is a hot, lead bullet.
Like all beautiful losers
Thorn has his stories;
he knows the winning horses' names
the triumphant combinations
the virtues of camouflage
the Powers and Dominions
of cocaine.
Like all abandoned angels
he fears entropy.
He says a wall withdraws
each time he quits the edge
when famished for velocity
he dislocates
into something strange.
When his head –
a meteor –
ignites the air
and his thoughts fall –
an abrasive rain.
I see him seized
in Disorder's beak
abducted, sacked
torn limb to limb.
I see his wheel
hanging lonely
in a flowering tree;
his fix
something mythical
clawing out
the eyes of
Daylight.

I watch, mazed and riddled
as before my eyes Thorn Falconer
is transformed to lizard.
He speeds
beneath the milky
blueprints of Heaven
to shelter
where he wages war
and worships Motion.
Suspended between
the cliff
and the dead river
he listens to the quarrels
of planets
and the laughter
of cut stones.
The days reel past:
Days of the Dog
Days of the Lizard
Days, sharp days, of glass.
Thorn Falconer
teaches me
the meaning of helplessness
the colours of desolation
the feel of Hell.
As he quickens to
transparency
I explore the rubble canyons
alone.
I haunt the heartland.
I have seen
the iron-vaulted
corridors of ants,
the eight-eyes
of the spider
sparked with foam.

The cool faces
of toy dragons
are magnified beneath my glass:
each bead –
each moon – a measure
of diminishing chances.
I keep company
to toads and vipers
scorpions and crickets
glass snakes and hornets.
I attend to the wilderness
in myself.

All things succumb to Seizure:
with a throttled stammer
a continent falters.
Like a house of paper aces
the familiar spaces
are plundered and flung down.
Love's shadow darts –
small leaps of faith –
from rock to rock.
In the distance
sometimes I think I see
Thorn Falconer stagger
beneath a sky convulsed
by too much magic.
Bottled devils in his pockets
white rattlesnakes and blue
straining on their leashes of sand.

III. DEVIL'S WANDS

Come spring the body of the Nereis is larded with grenades.
Too heavy to swim she hangs hooked to the skin of the sea.
Close by the male churns a whirlpool. He is a living
rainbow – yellow, red and green. He is a coil of desire,
a dervish wand, a liquid flame. And she, the Image of
Fullness, she is a time fuse. Her eggs are ticking.

When he approaches she explodes and the world rains
ovum and sperm.

Their fragmented bodies are dispersed by the tide.

Their pinprick children percolate like stars.

1 | DEVIL'S WANDS

Summers the lime tree is frosted with stick insects. Stick insects can sit still for hours at a time. And if I notice them at all, it is only because the tree is thick with egg-laying females. As I hear their eggs falling through the leaves, I look up expecting rain. Here they call them: *Les Bâtons du Diable*: Devil's wands.

2 | ANTLER BEETLES

The first year I came here, antler beetles scuttled across the lawn, the porch, the garden walls. Since then the vine grower's pesticides have killed them all, but before this holocaust I saw the males congregate in a nearby wood to do war. The sound of their hundred antlers in collision was the sound of battling reindeer, only quieter.

3 | SNAILS

Snails are quiet and hermaphrodite. After rain they come together, paddlers in a sexual pool, and face to face the one fecundates the other. The little pearly eggs, magically infused with light, tumble to the ground – the soaked moons of some other, smaller universe. Moons in the image of snails.

4 | WEEVILS DANCE FOR LOVE

Like cranes and storks (and for that matter, *all* the birds),
weevils dance for love. Silverfish quiver like iron filings
pursued by magnets. The male traces a diagram for the
female in perfumed ink – a silver road threading to the
four corners of the Treasure: sperm billowing beneath the
sink in volatile pyramids.

5 | FLOWERING LAVENDER

Every summer I lean over the flowering lavender watching
the tiger swallowtails and the bees – especially the tiny,
grey Italians, so nervous, so irritable, noisy as hornets –
drinking nectar. Once I saw a queen fly home with the
shreds of a lover's abdomen wagging from her body like a
flag.

Today I see a small, jade-coloured spider inflated with eggs.
Her eyes are soldered together in a tiara of black diamonds.
She crouches in the lavender on her haunches like a cat.
She allows me to breathe all over her, to count her eyes,
to admire a balloon-belly slashed with orange lightning.
Later, Venus and Jupiter shining low in the East and
Neptune in the West, I meet one of her relatives so pale as
to be transparent. She is as humped as a camel. She is no
bigger than the eye of a needle.

6 | THE LACE-WING

The lace-wing is also very cat-like when she scrubs her
green antennae clean. A cat-gazelle is what she is and leggy.
I wish I were small enough to caress her vaulted spine in
the place I imagine she'd like best. Just under the wings.

7 | THE PORCH LIGHT

I *have* caressed the toad who lives under the vine leaves beside the front door. My toad has no love life. He is weary of clinging to the nodular rumps of frantic giantess females. He spends his nights snapping at flies and staring in Amazement at the Glories of the Gnosis in the shape of Perfect Soul – the overhead porch light.

8 | AND OBELISKS

Everybody knows,that apes defend their territory by brandishing erections. It is their way of saying: *This place is mine.* Like the virile Hermes planted at crossroads and the entrances to Roman cities. And menhirs. The wands of wizards. The brooms of witches. The sceptres of kings. And obelisks.

9 | IF YOU BURN THEIR STEMS

If you burn their stems, poppies hold themselves together long enough to be painted. The poppy has its own fauna – black bugs not much bigger than grains of pepper. When the bugs are not climbing up and down the furry ladders of the stems, they sit on the petals facing the sun like seedlings.

There are three houses in my corner of the world cleaved from the village by vineyards and, in this season, a shimmering strip of sunflowers. My house with its toad, porch light and lime tree faces Southeast.

A neighbour who raises bees tells me that for bees East is best. He has planted a garden of melliferous plants: thyme, rosemary, lavender, clover, honeysuckle. His hives, as his house, face East. Those Italian bees I watch are his.

Lisette faces West. Sprightly despite a dowager's hump, she has flowers in all seasons. In the late afternoons of January when the sour, thorny plums are ripening above the road, she sets out pots of forced narcissi to catch the eye of the setting sun. In early August she has lilies tall as men. Her pears ripen in bottles like toy boats. And when a fragrant steam vaults the hedges which divide her property from mine, I know currants are being coaxed into jelly thick enough to be sliced. Our three houses are built of a calciferous, fossil-studded stone which subdues the sun as it reflects it. The entire sky is as tender and luminous as the belly of a river fish.

11 | A DEVIL-CHASER

Lisette is hedged in by her wild roses and a low, tumbledown wall of friable stone crowned with millepertuis: *fugga demonium* – The Devil Chaser! When I ask her if she needs a 'Devil Chaser' her girlish, wanton laughter takes me by surprise.

12 | MEN

Men, Lisette says it
Men are no better than what the cat brings in.

Her own cat is in the garden straining against gravity.
Lovers squabble in the ditch. The taker is one-eared and
piebald. He ambles over to her tight and loose together
like an experienced gambler.

When he seizes her by the neck she deflates like a paper
bag.

13 | A WIDOWER FACING NORTH

Lisette has lived alone ever since her husband ran off
with the green-groceress, *a bottle-brunette*. But lately she
has been hiding her hump beneath a scalloped shawl. It
crosses her back like canary-yellow wings. I see her, cane
in hand, nodding and tapping up the hill to the *coiffeur,
dames* where impoverished and bibbed in a barber chair
her white hair is tinted a very pale azure.

Lisette's man is a widower who lives on the hill facing
North. He gets all the wind but theirs is a summer affair.
He is a wizard, and despite great age continues to drive
a beautifully waxed Peugeot. He is famous for having
devitalized a difficult hex involving the death of many
cows. Balls of horsehair, crooked pins and upholsterer's
tacks were retrieved from the cow's multiple stomachs in
astonishing quantities.

14 | A MIRROR

The Peugeot is waxed to a purple shine. When the wizard
shows me its impeccable seat-covers I catch a glimpse of
my own face in the rear-view mirror. It is like the face
of an insect trapped beneath a lens; a lonely face. And
bodiless.

15 | DESPITE THE DRYNESS

Despite the dryness the eggplants in Lisette's garden are
enormous and as purple as her jam. She tells me her
lover prepares them himself in olive oil and lemon-juice
and garlic; he can't seem to get enough of them. And that
ever since the fruit has ripened, the cat – fine at moling
(something rare in cats) – refuses to go into the garden.
Lisette has seen a mole and mole-crickets. Has the wizard
hexed her cat? If so, *tant pis*, she confides: she'll *break off*.

An unusually hefty garden snake discovered nesting
beneath the over-turned wheelbarrow justifies the cat's
terror and assures the wizard's engagement.

16 | I FIND AN ALMOND

I find an almond in the road beneath an almond tree.
I run home for a large basket and fill it to the brim. A
luxury for the fall, the pelted fruit huddles like mite
animals. Later I discover these almonds are, like certain
memories, bitter.

17 | INFIDELITY

In the early afternoon Lisette and I are sipping cups
of tea. The Bee Man brings us new honey and pollen
fresh from the hive. As the chewy grains riot in our
unexperimented mouths, he tells us his wife has left him.
Familiar with bees and their moods as various as weather,
he has never come to grips with his wife. Her infidelity –
she has run off with the ginger-bearded motorcyclist we
have all seen parked in the woods nearby – stings worse
than anything, although it is true that the bees have
also mortified him. But when he peels off his shirt and
indicates a few discolourations, it is a tattoo which seizes
our imaginations.

It is a full-coloured tattoo representing four feral tigers
chasing one another's tails and comprised in a fiery wheel
of indigo-bodied hornets chasing *their* tails. The Bee Man
flexes his muscles. We learn that his wife hates the tattoo.
   'She calls this vulgar!' He spits angrily between his
shoes but we can see that he is crying. 'You can't tell me
this is more vulgar than a motorcycle.' He prods a tiger
with his thumb. 'What's more vulgar than a motorcycle?'

18 | A VERY FINE DITCH

Beneath Lisette's garden there is a very fine ditch; and
if she no longer has crayfish, Lisette has bullfrogs. She
has the first blossoming *ellebore* and later daisies by the
bunch.

I have a stone Lisette gave me because I admired it: a slab
of rust-coloured feldspar which lay in her petunia bed
for countless years, too heavy to move, offending her
sense of proportion and reminding her of her wayward
husband, a brooder. The Bee Man gets it to my place in
Lisette's wheelbarrow. When I offer him a glass of wine
for his trouble he says cryptically that someday soon he'd
like me to see his fish.

The stone is not as still as it looks. The surface is covered
with forests, a scaly magenta tundra, gold-leaf stars and
what look like fossil rivers, a little like the rivers of Mars.
I've counted twelve different things walking on it in as
many minutes. A small sort of fly hovers over it in the
afternoon creating what must be – for one pin-headed
spider – a very large shadow.

20 | A ROBBER'S MASK

I've been drawing capricorn beetles. The spots on
their backs vary tremendously and make up a species
of alphabet or code: two finger-tip spots, one robber's
mask, two coins; two finger-tip spots, one robber's mask
with horns, two coins; two finger-tip spots joined to a kite,
a bat wing, two coins; sometimes there are four coins and
sometimes no coins and instead two diamonds, or a disc,
or a disc like a flying saucer, its landing-gear unfolded.

In the centre of the village green stands an obelisk erected
to honour the First World War dead. A stone carver
curiously named Pierre Taillepierre had survived the
war to cut forty-four names into the stone – the names
of nearly all the men in the village, and those of his own
relatives and friends.

At the war's end six fellows too feeble to have participated
in the shellings and gassings, a nitwit who passed on last
winter, the pharmacist who had seizures and was not fit for
service and a pride of boys met Pierre and the two other
survivors – the beautiful Beaufreton twins – at the train
station. A large crowd of girls and women showed up too.

Pierre Taillepierre, Max and Alex Beaufreton repopulated
the village with bastards as well as legitimate sons and
daughters. Today in a village of one-hundred and
fifty people, seventy-nine are Beaufretons, fifty are
Taillepierres and as Lisette had pointed out, the others,
with other names, all share a resemblance with the twins'
or the stonecutter's descendance.

The three men precipitated many more sons than
daughters which is perhaps unnatural. Such potency has
provoked a superstitious fascination for the obelisk and its
sinister glyphs. Each year a bus parks on the green facing,
as if challenging, the memorial. Sterile women wanting
sons stumble out. They cross the green to finger the
incised stone. The wizard claims that the clump of grass
about the obelisk's base generates a not negligible quantity
of what he calls: 'static magnetism'.

These days every home boasts a television and the
flickering full-blooded bodies of Russian bears and
Chinese flag-dancers are beamed by satellite into all
the kitchens. When Lisette and I reach the green where
a family circus has planted a tiger cage and a tent, we
count twelve other people: all old women with their
littlest grandchildren. The surprisingly sleek tigers have
just been fed drugged meat. As they lie embracing they
purr so loudly we lift our faces to the sky craning for the
airplane which is not there.

23 | ERZSÉBET BÁTHORY

A sticky-looking arrow invites us into the rear-end
of a truck. Behind peep-holes of dusty glass we see
Urbain Grandier on fire, Gilles de Rais gazing into
the mismatched eyes of a decapitated infant, an Aztec
sacrifice and Erzsébet Báthory sticking pins into the arms
of a frantic child draped in artfully disarranged rags –
much like those Alice Liddell wore when she posed for
Charles Dodgson. A moth explores the victim's brilliantly
illuminated face.

The last peep-hole, the most mysterious of all, is
obscured with black tape. I am enchanted, but Lisette
barks: *Highway robbery!*

For the price of a new ticket we are promised acrobats.
We enter the tent and sit gingerly down on the ancient
benches. Within an instant the infants pick up splinters.

Just as Lisette notices that the tent has been repaired with
a singed electric blanket, we recognize the person who
sold us our tickets – dressed in a bathing suit and walking
towards us on her hands. As the children shriek she
pulls six eels from a tub of water and wraps them around
her neck. And she dances. We receive her dance with a
shudder and a surge of loneliness. When she eclipses,
bowing off backwards, two fat girls cartwheel forth in red
and green striped flannels. For ten minutes, an eternity,
they juggle green and red striped rubber balls creating,
says Lise, an extreme queasiness.

Lisette exults in irreverent cracks. Tonight she suggests
in a whisper that the World Itself is kept spinning by the
acrobatic efforts of some monstrous girl lying flat on her
back.

But there is magic in the wings. The lights, such as they
are, are dimmed. Way at the top of the tent a spot hits a
highwire and we see a stunning youth sitting on a silver
swing in an astonishing, white, sequin-studded leotard.
He heaves himself out over our heads and slides into
the air like a fish. Lise asks, *Who is he?* The Eel-Dancer's
lover? The young husband of one of the fat girls? With
tremendous sexual urgency and a kind of savage grace,
he leaps from his swing and hits the wire which sings.
Again he throws himself into the air where he appears
to hover like a neon sign or a comet pulsing. He is an
areal garden; he pirouettes, turns somersaults; he rides
a silver unicycle up and down the wire juggling bottles of
champagne and torches of fire. When he pulls a cork with
his teeth there is an explosion and the world rains wine.
As we applaud – and the little ones are weeping with
excitement – he flashes a smile as dazzling as his sequins
and his act.

Monday morning over the hedge Lisette and I tell the Bee Man about the acrobat.

'Acrobats, Motorcyclists,' he pontificates, 'people such as that all end up dead. Sequins!' he spits. Winnowing under his shirt he scratches the belly of a hornet and yawns in disgust.

'He was wonderful.' Lisette insists. 'He looked like Alex Beaufreton.'

'Wasn't Alex a twin?' I ask. 'How did he differ from his brother?'

'Alex had the fire.'

Once we are alone she continues: 'If I was forty-five years younger I know what I'd do. You're young enough for that acrobat, she says, 'I hope for your sake he'll be back.' But the circus comes only this one time.

27 | FREAKED PARTICLES

Talking to the Bee Man and listening to the wind, the woodwinds of the insects, the zithers, papered combs and fiddles. He says he's noticed how butterflies all travel in zig zags of varying intervals; he thinks if he could chart these patterns on tracing paper and superpose them, he'd learn something even the physicists don't know about freaked particles.

'It would be seeing in four dimensions!' he exclaims. 'Think of the zig as positive and the zag as negative ... I'd like to show you something.' He takes me upstairs. I expect to see butterflies; instead I see an arcane collection of stuffed fish. Mounted on plywood and hung from the ceiling, they navigate in an eerie blue atmosphere which brings to mind poison gas.

The wizard has been seen picking mushrooms with another lady. I take Lisette to Paris where she's never been. She's brought along bottled water.

'My head doesn't stay the same when I take the train,' she says, and taking a swig from the bottle which may be laced with *eau de vie* adds, 'Ever since their second war I think of trains as sinister.'

We visit the botanical gardens. Beyond the muted glass the sun shines green. But when we take the path which leads to the museum of Natural History, the horizon turns purple, the sky orange and hail the size of marbles tumbles to the bronze backs of dinosaurs and Buffon's bronze head.

Inside the museum the universe is cool and dim. It is also empty and ours. We pass case after case of the Very First Things, magical, not exactly animal, not quite vegetable, nor mineral – but gifted with the essential instincts, eager for life, eager to try out its infinite combinations. Lise and I move up the chain from simple to complex in the blinking of an eye.

'Our ancestors,' she scowls, 'look sinister too.' And suddenly they do. Perhaps we feel the loneliness of beings who, having resolved the enigma of our origins and unable to look upon ourselves as special children, have broken the chain and created the haemorrhage.

White as our houses and friable, the fossils lie like the sightless skulls of some unknown and diminutive species.

IV. THE ANIMALS PAINTED BY ALOYS ZÖTL

ALOYS ZÖTL was born in Bohemia on the thirteenth of April, 1803. From 1832 to 1887 – the year of his death – he painted 170 achingly beautiful water-colours of animals often inhabiting the ideal landscapes of his imagination. Years were kingdoms: 1832 ruled by fish, 1835 by reptiles, 1837 by the gentle tyranny of birds. André Breton called his bestiary 'the most sumptuous ever seen.'

I |

These are the seasons of my infancy
seized in the painter's perfect ice
and their cries, their open faces
animate the gardens I have lost.
I think of them as keys –
entire alphabets.

These are the seasons of my most precious past
the breathing waters of my dreams;
spirit given fur, a throat and wings;
These are my first imaginings –
visions through the looking glass
of an entire, faultless air.

2 |

I have seen them in gardens
carved at the foothills of childhood.
Nut brown with golden manes
I have seen them hiding
behind the tense wands of trees
like four-footed memories.

The colour of bruised plums
I have seen them tempting the sky
blazing like one thousand suns
slipping through the finger of prehistory.
A living kindling
reinstating wildness.

3 |

Now I remember the way it was dwelling in fullness.
How turtles – the mighty houses of magic hammered to
their backs –
breathed above the breathing waters.
How ibises – redder than hieroglyphs stained with blood –
beaked the air revealing angels.
How bulls, hot and hoofed, kicked up a secret dust.
When horns ruled the moon.

I remember how monkeys leapt like acrobats
and demonstrated tricks with staves.
How – when it was the frog's turn to dream the world –
it rained and rained.
On violent nights the hyenas conjured hurricanes
and as cobras kept the halls of royal graves
fish fascinated waves.
You see: even their saliva contains a special knowledge;
their voices (barkings, trillings, croakings) cast spells.

Yes, now I remember: They are all the orders of the angels.

4 |

When I met Death
summer was a tiger
breathing down my neck.
And Death was dizzy with bees;
Death was metallic.

Waiting in green leaves
Death wore the red of the fox;
the gold nugget bees
swarmed at Death's heart.
Death's blood was black.

Startled, I stepped back
into a sudden confinement.
Now I know the colour of Death's season:
gold, red and green.
Death's tongue is black.

5 |

Give me a burrow lined with silk
a starless place to overwinter.
Give me eyes, eight dreamless eyes
honed for clarity like knives
an anaesthetic milk and owl-light.
Give me a well and a voice
like a clapperless bell.
Give me the weedy margins,
the damp woods and attic windows
gardens and green stems.
Give me the morning
closets and vertical cliffs.
Give me the weather
and I shall noose the wind
and weave the air with spiderlings
and prowl the mouth of the wolf
to seize his bark
and blind, by touch
confront the dark.

6 |

As the moon strikes the hours and the chiming sun –
everywhere, my heart, the animals are burning.
What are fur and feathers but tubes of air feeding fire
the leopard's spots the fire marks of greedy constellations;
the zebra's coal-black zodiac bruises of the Devil's stick.
Even the ibis swarms with demons small as atoms of air.
Everywhere, my heart, the animals are burning.
As their names go up in smoke I gag on chips of bone.

As Ubaner – cuckold and necromancer – lies with his
wife, she cries out in pleasure. She calls him: Al-Awwal
(The First) and Al-Akhir (The Last) and even Al-Wâhid
(The One). But Ubaner hears the silent cry of her heart:
Al-Bâtin (The Hidden).

Ubaner makes a crocodile of wax. Although his wife
protests he confiscates her needles for the creature's
teeth, and although she is weeping, removes her yellow-
ruby earrings. He needs them for the monster's eyes.

When Ubaner is satisfied that the crocodile is perfect he
carries it down to the river. He lays it in the water and
names it: Al-Mûmit (The Quickener). His wife crouches
in the mud sobbing.

Once the figure is submerged, wax quickens to flesh.
Before the crocodile swims away it flashes a smile
brimming with needles at Ubaner.

In no time, the creature slams into the lover's chamber
tearing up a carpet in its haste. Its eyes are horribly
familiar. 'Who are you?' the doomed man asks. 'I am Al-
Muntakim!' barks the beast. 'The Avenger!'

Indeed, had the bleeding victim taken the time to look,
he would have seen that his assassin is brown, the colour
of dead leaves – the colour of penitence and grief, ruin
and decay.

8 | THE FROG

Spitting salt and bile, Ubaner's wife sinks into the Nile's blue mud. It is the last time the wizard sees her; incessant weeping has transformed her into a frog.

As Ubaner throws himself in an agony of impotent love upon a slab of bone-dry alabaster, she – her skin splashed a treacherous yellow – gazes off in the opposite direction. She has spotted a male member of her species stalking gnats in the grass.

Ubaner – widower and necromancer – sits in his boat attempting to read his destiny in a pool of violet ink as it evaporates in the palm of his hand. Being a careless man – and even more so since his wife's metamorphosis – Ubaner has chosen Saturday, that exemplary day of misadventure characterized by lead. Captivated by the ink he does not see that both the water and the sky have assumed the cast of that unauspicious metal.

In a boat the colour of dead leaves, Ubaner, who wears the pale blue turban of chaste affection, is quite suddenly crushed to death by an orange boa with a mouth like a coffin of needles. The snake has thrown itself into the boat from an overhanging branch.

In a happier moment Ubaner might have told us that orange, bitter orange, is the livery of passion and that white – especially when it is peerless as the boa's belly – *always* signifies death.

In his youth it had occurred to Ubaner that just as the anagrammatic alphabets of magicians have since the distant past been inscribed in clay or painted on papyrus or silk, or as with the Gnostics and the Greeks carved into carnelians, or, as in Persia, painted on the skins of foetal gazelles – so the writing of Heaven appears on the hides and scales and feathers of animals. And as the spells of wizards are transmitted in writing from one generation to the next, so the animal's offspring transmit the sacred texts.

The stripes of zebras, the spots of leopards and giraffes, the masks of bears and parrots, the little owl netted in wavelets, the relic stain down the antelope's back (all that remains of a bristling mane) – are alive with esoteric meanings, the initials of the names of archons and angels, the abbreviations of cosmic formulae.

'Animals,' Ubaner had liked to tell his wife, 'carry their amulets directly on their bodies just as Egyptian children wear at their throats that violet stone which, as everyone knows, is the substantialization of the tears Eve shed when she was exiled forever from Eden.'

THE DEEP ZOO
Two Essays

SILLING

Sade completed "that most impure tale" — and the words are his — *The 120 Days of Sodom* — in the Bastille where he was confined for infractions that, if they were outrageous, were not murderous and — unlike civilians in wartime — involved consenting adults. Sade was an outspoken atheist, a libertine and a sodomist at a moment in history when sodomy was punishable by a public breaking of the offending body on the wheel. *The 120 Days* was a purposeful declaration of war against those who would never cease to persecute its author for his singularity. Like a suicide bombing, it is a cry of rage and a rending of the veil; it is an act of defiance and morbidity, the wilful embrace of the role of the bogeyman — whose arbitrary and inescapable destiny is acute humiliation and a horrendous death.

The 120 Days is so relentlessly obscene that Sade himself declared he hadn't the stomach to revise it. Yet, when on the 14th of July the Bastille was stormed and it seemed the manuscript was lost, he "shed tears of blood" and this because, despite its flaws, he knew he had achieved his object: he had written a book that would never cease to do violence to its author and to the world simultaneously. And yet this novel, unlike any other, also provides a place of reflection (Sade always demands a great deal of *reflection* from his readers) and, for those who share his anomalous vertigo, sexual restlessness, perhaps release. Sade's brand of restlessness, however, provokes moral disquiet, and, for all its flamboyance, *The 120 Days* is less a pillow book than a novel of distopia. Its manic restlessness and lethal mockeries all lead to a question whose answer was a matter of urgency for Sade himself and is, more than ever, a matter of urgency for us all:

> Why is it ... that in this world there are men whose hearts have been so numbed, whose sentiments of honour and delicacy have been so deadened, that one sees them pleased and amused by what degrades and soils them? (492)

In other words, Sade who wrote *the most impure tale that has ever been told since the world began* (253), a book that was the measure of the horror that would, in the name of brotherhood, drench Paris with blood, was on to something. *The 120 Days* is not only a rageful (and at times rueful) procession of the author's own determinisms, it is a mirror of Hell — 600 crimes! — and like Jenin — where this morning as I write, Palestinian civilians are digging in the rubble for their dead — a Hell of human manufacture. One man's imaginary war zone, *The 120 Days* offers an occasion for necessary thoughtfulness. This is, unexpectedly, a moral novel. Sade called it his *Book of Sorrows*.

◆

The 120 Days of Sodom opens thus:

> The extensive wars wherewith Louis XIV was burdened during his reign, while draining the state's treasury and exhausting the substance of the people, nonetheless contained the secret that led to the prosperity of a swarm of those bloodsuckers who are always on the watch for public calamities, which, instead of appeasing, they promote or invent so as, precisely, to be able to profit from them the more advantageously. (191)

Sade's satirical intention cannot be clearer. He continues:

One must not suppose that it was exclusively the low born and vulgar
sort which did this swindling; gentlemen of the highest note led the
pack. (191)

Sade next offers up his *champions*, the *four bloodsuckers* and
traffickers who will *assume the major roles in these unusual orgies*, orgies
that will take place in the faraway castle of Silling. They are:
The Duc de Blangis and his brother the Bishop of X***
(a nobleman, therefore, and a man of the church), the
celebrated Durcet and the Président de Curval (business
and secular authority. How much fun Sade would have
had with Enron, the current scandals rocking the Catholic
church, the skeletons that continue to kick in Kissinger's
closets!)

Now let us examine, beneath Sade's burning glass, his
four uncharitable and immutable villains, *ces messieurs* who
will live out their errant, their costly lusts, in Silling.

First of all, the Duc de Blangis, the inheritor of
immense wealth has been endowed by nature *with every impulse,*
every inspiration required for its abuse. What's more, he was:
Born treacherous, harsh, imperious, barbaric, selfish... (he is) *a liar,*
a gourmand, a drunk, a dastard, a sodomite, fond of incest, given to
murdering, to arson, to theft...(198). His brother, the Bishop of
X***, *has the same black soul, the same penchant for crime, the same*
contempt for religion, the same atheism, the same deception and cunning
(203). Our financier, Durcet's loftiest pleasure is *to have his*
anus tickled by the Duc's enormous member (210) (speculators have
always been tickled by inherited wealth). Finally — and I
have purposefully saved the Président de Curval for last
— we come to this *pillar of society worn by debauchery to a singular*
degree (205) and who is little more than a skeleton caked
with shit. Curval is exemplary of Sade's emblematic, self-
hating, pleasure-fearing endeavour. He surges throughout
the novel in various guises — for example *the man from Roule*
who fucks in shrouds and coffins and who, familiar with the idea of death
(is) *hence unafraid of it* (505). A sentiment familiar to those

who have read the tales of torturers whose *little ceremonies* make them feel more virile, more alive, even immortal. Like all men who torture, Sade's champions are fearful of the body and its determinisms: shit, sex and death, and so must *shiver* it, reduce it from three dimensions to two, make it into meat:

Frigs the whore's clitoris ... chops it up with a knife ... (582)

and in this way demonstrate it never had any meaning, any *individuality* (Silling's slaves are silenced, reduced to dumb beasts; their tongues may be cut out, their mouths sewn shut). Silling's victims are emptied out and flattened — as some would do to an entire country in order to establish that it was never there.

Back to Curval. He is *entirely jaded.* He is, as was Sade, nearly impotent, and needs nearly *three hours of excess, and the most outrageous excess ... before one could hope to inspire a voluptuous reaction in him* (206). Already dead, animated by fantastications and the unlimited power Silling affords him, Curval frolics in the boneyards of his making and leaps to a particularly inspired *danse macabre.* He embodies all of Sade's libertines for whom the spasms of orgasm and the death throes converge. This convergence never ceases to throb at the icy core of *The 120 Days* and to propulse an extremity of longing that, as time passes, seems less a boast and more a possibility:

Ah, how many times, by God, have I not longed to be able to assail the sun, snatch it out of the universe, make a general darkness, or use that star to burn the world. (364)

The promise of *general darkness,* is the shadow beneath which the universe of Silling leans into entropy, a faded universe, its ancient machinery — space and time — grinding to a deafening halt, yet capable of igniting in one last hideous conflagration. Masters of space, Curval and the other champions toil, with furious detachment, on the side of Time; they excel in the service of its machinations. Their little ceremonies assure an eternity of agony, and paradoxically, precipitous death. (Most of the victims of Silling are very young.) As the old saw would have it, money buys time; Curval is filthy rich and it is wealth, Sade reminds us, that enables him and the others to indulge in *unusual pastimes*. Excessive wealth makes all our Sillings possible. It buys U.S. F-16s and Apache helicopters.

♦

Like the *One Thousand and One Nights*, *The 120 Days* is propelled by stories. Radical and inexorable malice is assured by the virago storytellers' unavoidable soliloquies that, *decorated with numerous and searching details ... apt to have an immense influence* (271) commence punctually at six o'clock, like the evening news. The storytellers are *moulins à paroles* — word mills — whose narrations keep the mill of death oiled with cum and ceaselessly wheeling. Like the ogresses of fairytales or the winds of war, their mills grind bones. The sounds of bones breaking castanet the air, as do, with whorlwindish velocity, the champions' groans. To keep the mill turning, the four agree to banish rational thinking from Silling and to replace it with the logic of nightmare:

> *Any friend ... who may take it into his head to act in accordance with a single glimmer of common sense ... shall be fined ten-thousand francs.* (248)

— a rule that could have been invented by Robespierre (who sent lace-makers to the guillotine for practicing a frivolous craft), Sharon (who, as I write, will not allow ambulances into places he has besieged, nor allow for the burial of the dead), and our own President, for that matter, so eagerly gearing up for a war with Iraq.

When coupling — and their couplings are hectic and meticulous — the *Messieurs*, their jaded imaginations ignited by the storytellers' descriptions of bodies *reduced to scarlet shambles* (463), *of pricks stabbed with a heavy cobbler's awl* (409), *of bone-shattering cuffs* (459) are incapable of not only compassion but erotic delight; they collide into the bodies of those they hold in thrall like tanks slamming into kitchens. Is it surprising, then, that they like to dine on shit? In Silling, sexuality is the embodiment of fury, a bloody theatre, an act of terror. Like a species of athanor in reverse, Silling transmutes everything into lead.

◆

You will recall that in his *Grounding for the Metaphysics of Morals*, Kant proposes that each one of us *always act in such a way that you can also will that the maxim of your action should become universal law* (V). It is evident that for the individual with a will to do good, Kant's criterion affords a rigorous practice in moral living, one that, above all, demands a searching conscience and fearless inquisitiveness, and the willingness to restlessly question dogmatic thinking — one's own and that of others — to engage in, and tirelessly, a process of disenthrallment.

Sade's Silling offers a Manichean reversal and negation of such a moral practice. In Silling, Libertine Law, Universal Law and the Law of Nature are one and the same. The friends are simply acting as Nature intends: brutal and blind — Sade an anti-Rousseau (although he did admire that *threat for dull-witted bigots!*) and, curiously, very much in keeping with the teachings of the Inquisition which, fed by stories of naked New Worlders worshipping devils and buggering one another, argue that nature, a satanic realm studded with glamours and perversions, demons in the shapes of bears, wenches and wolves, the semen of frogs and serpents teased into malefic powers — leads straight to madness. Such pessimism evokes a radical Gnosticism, proclaiming as it does man's active place in a scheme of chronic pain and interminable night. Sade's Nature knows nothing of pity and is forever tormenting her creatures with plagues and mortifications; later, in *Juliette* Sade will write: *are plants and animals acquainted with mercy, pity ... brotherly love?* (888)

Sade, always paradoxical, offers up this curiosity; he both despises the church and its stultifying myths, yet climbs into bed with a churchy arsenal of crucifixes and wafers and, when it comes to Nature, embraces with a vengeance the Catholic world view at its most extreme; an awkward backwardness for a man who was in so many ways a radical thinker — a champion of female sexuality, a vociferous detractor of the guillotine. In an earlier age the four libertines of Silling would have been witches.

I recall a story by the Belgian writer of fantasy, Jean Ray, in which a diabolical house — much like the Aztec universe — demands to be fed fresh corpses. Silling is such a place. And *ces messieurs* are famished; their famishment, too, is cosmical. They would take on everything, even the weather:

> *He passes an entire brothel in review; he receives the lash from*
> *all the whores while kissing the madame's arsehole and receiving*
> *therefrom into his mouth both wind and rain and hailstones.* (584)

Such a madame, one supposes, can be nothing but the embodiment of Mother Nature.

◆

When the four reach Silling, they destroy the bridge that allows them access and once inside decide

> ... it were necessary ... to have walled shut all the gates, and all the passages whereby the château might be penetrated, and absolutely to enclose themselves inside their retreat as within a besieged citadel, without leaving the least entrance to an enemy, the least egress to a deserter ... They barricade themselves to such an extent there was no longer any trace of where the exits had been; and they settled down comfortably inside. (240-241)

Tomb, gnostical world hermetically sealed, Silling is colonized like a defeated country, and like terrorized civilians its slaves are given two choices only: to be corrupted (some like certain survivors of Auschwitz become accomplices) or to submit. All resistance, imaginary and fabricated (the slaves are given emetics and forbidden to shit) is punished by torture and execution. Never does good resist evil; it is as if Sade cannot conceive it, as if helplessness and passivity serve as puissant aphrodisiacs. Then, again, the victims have always been figments only, flat, with no minds of their own. Silling, is, after all, a Looking Glass world; the world of the Red Queen whose vassals are merely cards. Among the vast store of things the four friends have brought with them are *many mirrors;* Silling, you understand, is the mirror of our most acute failures: a city under siege, a country burning with no road leading out, a place of perfect moral isolation. If I have chosen to evoke Sade's sinister castle in this essay, it is not only because Silling's mirror of bloody ink affords an exhaustive inquiry into what a world ruled by killers is like, but because it is Silling's *banality,* after all, that should make us shudder, not its singularity.

Fantasy allows the reader to burn her own bridges and continue the tale *à sa guise,* to, in Sade's own words, *sprinkle in whatever tortures you like* (671). Silling is potentially everyman's fable, mirror, tomb. And if one has read *The 120 Days* to the bitter, the ironical end, has one at any moment been complicitous? Has one dared acknowledge and investigate this complicity? Has the reader sprinkled in whatever tortures she likes? Or was she made too ill to think and did she turn her head away in disgust? Fatal mistake! Or will she, will we, take up Silling's challenge and offer a refutation? One that does not entail *melting our enemies' cities*, as some fool recently proposed in *The Denver Post* — a jaded response that embraces Silling's vertiginous bestiality, Sade's own longing for cosmical conflagrations. What is needed, of course, is far less simple (and shall take much more than *a single glimmer of common sense!*); it depends upon a painful and necessary disentanglement from fatal habits of mind, a lasting and muscled recognition of common humanity, an ordered, a passionate vision for global justice, a veritable *setting to rights*. Compassion — for those the hottest heads among us choose to call, without knowledge or distinction, "the enemy" — if it is to bring about peace, must be perceived as an active principle (unlike sentimentality which is, after all, simply another form of cowardice). In order to survive our next confrontation with Silling — the calamity we will suffer or inflict upon others, we will have to, each one of us, act in the manner Kant proposes and this if we are to, finally, overcome and abandon the pathology that dictates our unreason.

Silling, once seemingly so far, is now very close. If Sade has been so vilified — and, despite the vagaries of fashion will continue to be, just as he always risks being embraced for all the wrong reasons — it is because Silling has never been one man's uniquely aberrant vision, but a species of accelerated perspective, an anamorphosis that, when seen through the world's own looking glass, is recognizable. Silling, like Ground Zeros everywhere, like the killing fields that separate our country from our neighbour to the south, like our own densely populated penitentiaries, is simply another name for all our own worst mistakes. It is my conviction that had we dared read Sade rigorously, dared respond to the terrible questions he poses, we might have been prepared for the worst. Silling's fires continue to burn; they gather strength and momentum.

♦

Many years ago (this was in 1965) I was invited to have tea with the French wife of the American consul in Algeria. She received me, her face slathered in cream, in a room across the street from a notorious prison. I suggested that living in such close proximity to a place where so many Algerians had been tortured during the war for independence must be a cause for much distress. But no; she told me she'd had a maid tortured there herself, for stealing silverware. "But then," she laughed, "I *found* the silverware!"

Needless to say, I didn't stay for tea but left at once to learn soon after that the maid had been tortured so severely she had been crippled. The soles of her feet had been beaten to a pulp with heavy rods — a method perfected by the thugs of Francoist Spain. The consul's wife's allegresse reminds me of those criminally vapid presidential debates when Bush spoke so gleefully of the death penalty. In Curval's words:

Better everytime to fuck a man than seek to comprehend him. (496)

THE DEEP ZOO

Writing is the uncovering of that which was unrevealed.
— Ghani Alani, *Dreaming Paradise*

♦ In the tradition of Islam, the first word that was revealed to Mohammed was *Iqrá* (Read!) The world is a translation of the divine, and its manifestation. To write a text is to propose a reading of the world and to reveal its potencies. Writing *is* reading and reading a way back to the initial impulse. Both are acts of revelation.

♦ The Ottoman calligraphers delighted in creating mazes of embellishment in which the text was secreted like a treasure. The text needed to be deciphered and the task proved the worthiness of the reader. These calligrapher's mazes remind us that if the text is the mirror of an exorbitant, mutable universe, it is playful, too. The maze places the text within an intimate space, very like a garden, where the text hides, then reveals itself; perhaps it could be said such a text is *irresistible*. Writes Gaston Bachelard: *All the spaces of intimacy are designated by an attraction (Poetics of Space)*.

♦ The texts we write are not visible until they are written. Like a creature coaxed from out a deep wood, the text reveals itself little by little. The maze evokes a multiplicity of approaches, the many tricks we employ to tempt the text hither. The maze is both closed and open; it demands to be approached with a *thoughtful lightness* (Calvino). The powers lurking within it are like stars. Despite their age and inaccessibility, their light continues to reach us and to reveal us to ourselves.

♦ A playful mind is deeply responsive to the world and informed by powers instilled during infancy and childhood, powers that animate the imagination with primal energies. A playful mind is guided as much by attraction as consistency and coherence — and I am thinking here of Lewis Carroll's Looking Glass world — its consistent tyrants, the coherence of its nonsense and the energy of Alice's fearless lucidity. The Looking Glass reminds us that the world's maze is attractive to eager thinkers. After all, playfulness describes as much the scientist as the artist (and Lewis Carroll was both).

The idea that the world was engendered by the spoken word comes to us from Egypt. Here language flourished, mirroring and delighting in the phenomenal world. Here Paradise persisted; the gods and their creatures dwelling together in good understanding or, phrased differently, in *knowledge* of one another. And if the world of nature and its book indicated the divine, it also provided a place of unlimited encounters. To name a thing was to acknowledge and evoke its primary potencies — religious, medical and magical. Plants, minerals and animals were not only animated by the divine breath (*nous*), they were its vessels. Each tree, bird, river and star was an altar, the dwelling place of a god. To gaze upon the world's image reflected in the waters of the Nile was to gaze into and reflect upon a sacred face or body: Hathor the cow-faced goddess embodied by the moon, Horus, the falcon, perched among the reeds.

Deep in the desert, each fossil shell was seen as Hathor's gift, tossed to earth from the sky; the fossil sea urchin's five-pointed star needled to its back indicated its stellar origins and explains why such things are found placed near the dead in ancient tombs. To use a lovely term of Gaston Bachelard's, such a revery — and to leap from stone to star can only be called a revery — *digs life deeper, enlarge(s) the depth of life*. Bachelard offers these lines from the poet Vincent Huidobro:

In my childhood is born a childhood burning like alcohol.
I would sit down in the paths of night
I would listen to the discourse of the stars
And that of the tree.

— *The Poetics of Revery*

Such *sympathies* — the stone, the moon caught in the branches of the willow, the gods, the stars — are born of looking at the world and a deep dreaming. The ancient world of sympathies, rooted in inquisitiveness and informed by imaginative seeing, gave us marvellous aesthetic and scientific achievements; alchemy for example — that exemplary amalgam of science and poetry, that 'immense word revery' says Bachelard. It would be a mistake to dismiss such *sympathies* as mere foolishness, for they were born of qualities of mind that illustrate what Italo Calvino calls the *lightness of thoughtfulness (Six Memos for the Next Millennium)* and illumine his phrase: *poetry is the enemy of chance*. The moment one reaches for the star-struck stone, the revery begins; the moment its star is recognized as a piece of the night sky fallen to earth, the poem begins. Chance gives way to a deep seeing and the recognition of a pattern that informs the mind with light, a pattern that incandesces and *burns like alcohol*. If poetry is the enemy of chance, it is also *the daughter of chance*.

If I have chosen to open this essay with an evocation of an ancient world and its *sympathies*, it is because the urgencies concealed within the maze of the mind that animate our imaginations, provoke incandescence on the page. I am not calling for magical thinking, obscurity or preciousness, but for an eager access to memory, revery and the unconscious — its powers, beauties, terrors and, perhaps above all, its rule-breaking intuitions, and to celebrate with you the mind's longing to become lighter, free of the weight of received ideas and gravity-bound redundancies. If we were scientists and not writers, we would not waste our time re-inventing gravity. Speaking of a poet he especially admires, Calvino says:

> The miraculous thing about his poetry is that he simply takes the weight out of language to the point that it resembles moonlight.
> — Six Memos for the Next Millennium

And Bachelard:

> For things as for souls, the mystery is inside. A revery of intimacy — of an intimacy which is always human — opens up for the (one) who enters into the mysteries of matter.
> — The Poetics of Revery

The mysteries of matter are the potencies that in the shapes of dreams, landscapes, exemplary instants and so on inform our imagining minds; they are powers. For Bachelard they take the form of shells, a bird's nest, an attic; for Borges a maze, mirrors, the tiger; for Calvino moonlight, the flame and the crystal; for Cortazar ants on the march and the cry of the rooster.

Potencies are never static but in constant flux within our minds and what's more, they *fall in sympathy* with one another. For example, for Borges there is an evident sympathy between the tiger's stripes, the world's maze, language and the maze of the mind; for Calvino between moonlight and the lucent transparency of clear thinking; for Bachelard between attics and a love of solitude; for Cortazar between the cock's cry and the knowledge of mortality, of finitude.

◆

The world of animals is an ocean of sympathies from which we drink only drops whereas we could drain torrents from it.
> — Lamartine (as quoted by Giovanni Mariottini in
> his essay on Aloys Zötl, *F.M.R.* #1)

◆

One evening years ago, a family circus set up its shabby tent in the park of a French village — Le Puy Notre Dame in the Val de Loire — I called home. As I approached the park I heard the sound of a powerful motor and searched the sky for an airplane — a rarity at that time in that place. The sky was empty of everything, even clouds, and the thrumming I heard was the purring of tigers. An instant later I saw the cage and two exquisite tigers, surely drugged; their contentment in such small quarters was uncanny. If I recall this distant evening, its circus and its tigers for you now, it is in guise of an introduction to *potencies in the shape of beasts*.

For the first issue of Franco Maria Ricci's magazine *F.M.R.*, Julio Cortazar was asked to write an essay on the bestiary of a little known and eccentric 19th century painter from the foothills of the Bohemian mountains whose name is Aloys Zötl. From 1832 to 1887 — the year of his death — Zötl painted 170 achingly beautiful water-colours of animals inhabiting the ideal landscapes of his imagination. Years were kingdoms: 1832 ruled by fish, 1835 by reptiles, 1837 by the gentle tyranny of birds. André Breton called his bestiary 'the most sumptuous ever seen.'

Instead of describing Zötl's bestiary, Cortazar chooses to walk us through his own Deep Zoo. His essay is titled "A Stroll Among the Cages" and it is a parallel journey on a path *burning like alcohol* that generously leads straight to Cortazar's own holding ground of totems, just as it prepares our eyes for the sight to come: Zötl's lucent tigeries and tigered lucencies:

And then a cock crowed, if there is a memory it is because of that,
but there was no notion of what a cock was, no tranquilizing name,
how was I to know that was a cock, that horrible rending of the
silence into a thousand pieces, that shattering of space throwing its
tinkling glass down on me, a first and frightful Roc.

This shattering of silence precipitates the infant Cortazar into a waking nightmare that would never abandon him entirely. It informs the beasts that follow — with a vaguely menacing shimmer.

What comes next, writes Cortazar, *has a Guarani Indian name: mamboretá, a name that's long and beautiful just like its green and prickly body, a dagger that suddenly plunges into the middle of your soup or drops onto your cheek when the summer table is set ...* and there is always an aunt who flees in terror, and a father who authoritatively proclaims the inoffensive nature of the *mamboretá* while thinking, perhaps, but not mentioning the fact that the female devours the male in the midst of copulation. And Cortazar recalls the terrible moment when the *mamboretá would become enraged* with him for past torments and look at him from its branch, accusingly. Barking frogs come next (Zötl, by the way, was especially partial to frogs and the lion's part of his bestiary belongs to them), and swarming ants that *pass through a house like a detergent, like the fearsome machine of fascism,* locusts whose devastation brings Attila to mind, and a couple of amorous lions, their bodies trembling *slightly with the orgasm.* Cortazar fulfills his promise to us and admirably: we have strolled among the animals, although to tell the truth, there were no cages anywhere. The vision is clear, unobstructed and hot. Cortazar has given us totemic potencies; he has given us Aloys Zötl.

Now, because I cannot offer you Zötl's paintings and because Cortazar chose not to describe them, the task falls to me.

The imaging consciousness holds its object (such images as it imagines) in an absolute immediacy.
— Gaston Bachelard, *The Poetics of Revery*

Immediacy is precisely the word that characterizes Aloys Zötl's bestiary. With few exceptions, he had seen his subjects in books only, yet painted them with feverish deliberation. I imagine it was chronic and unrequited longing that drove him on, for his bestiary surges with all the kaleidoscopic opulence of a mushroom enhanced daydream. Spangled and lucent, Zötl's beasts have been conjured hair by hair; one can count their whiskers, their feathers and their teeth. (One thinks of Borges' magician dreaming hour after hour and one by one the infinite elements that make for a living man.) Zötl's creatures take their ease in gardens as lavish as wonder rooms; he has packed his pictures with rarities so that the overall effect recalls the haunting superabundance of Max Ernst's experiments with rough surfaces and sopping rags, those hieroglyphic landscapes haunted by hierophantic lop lops. Or Borgesian dream gardens which are the amalgam of all the gardens one has ever loved. Zötl's pictures provide a glimpse of paradise: it is a first glimpse, prodigal and unfettered. In other words, Zötl has painted the potencies of Old Time, when to name a thing was to bring it surging into the real. Even his scattered stones are poised for speech.

But — what about tigers? It seems there are none. However, there is a leopard, completed in April, 1837. He is the same leopard that haunts the fables of the Maya and, as all the rest, he is meticulously painted *and he is very still*. Clearly he has heard a sound that has frightened him. Perhaps he has heard, and for the first time, the crowing of a cock. And perhaps this is the writer's task: to make audible a sound of warning — which is also the sound of awakening.

◆

The subconscious is ceaselessly murmuring, and it is by listening to these murmurs that one hears the truth.

— Gaston Bachelard, *The Poetics of Revery*

Back to Egypt where things and their names were not seen as separate entities, but were instead in profound sympathy with one another. These perceived sympathies are often very playful, as in this story of Isis and Seth:

Seth, in the form of a bull, attempts to overcome Isis. Fleeing, she takes the form of a little dog holding a knife in its tail and evades him. In his thwarted excitement, Seth ejaculates and his seed spills to the ground.

When Isis sees this she cries: *What an abomination! To have thus scattered your seed!*

Where Seth's seed has fallen, a plant grows called the coloquint (or bitter apple). In ancient Egypt the word for *coloquint* and *your seed* is one and the same.

Within a writer's life, words, just as things, acquire powers. For Borges, *Red* is such a word, as is *Labyrinth* and *Tiger*. And if Beauty in the form of a yellow tiger or a red rose *waits in ambush for us* (*Seven Nights*), beautiful words are the mind's animating flame.

In his essay on his blindness, Borges recalls a cage he saw as a child holding leopards and tigers; he recalls that he *lingered before the tiger's gold and black*. Nearly blind he is no longer able to see red, *that great colour which shines in poetry, and which has so many beautiful names*, but it is the yellow of the tiger that persists, as does its beauty and the power of its beautiful name. In his story *The Zahir*, the Tiger *is* the Zahir; it is the face of God, God's name, the sound He uttered when He created the world, the *Shadow of the Rose* and the *rending of the Veil (Labyrinths)*. Tiger is the power that brings the unborn universe surging into the real and, what's more, it is the name of the infinite book you and I are writing; it is the letters of each word of this book; Tiger is the calligrapher's maze and also the text hidden within that maze.

It is the *shell* that tigers Bachelard — that lover of intimacy and solitude. A creature with a shell is a *mixed creature*; it reveals and conceals itself simultaneously. You will recall that in ancient times a fossil shell acquired the potencies of the moon. Stones of unusual shapes were empowered by Osiris also; they evoked the myth of his dismemberment and his own scattered limbs. In the myth, Isis gathers the pieces of her husband's broken body and makes him whole; she revives him. For Bachelard, *the fossil is not merely a being that once lived but one that is still asleep in its form.* He is speaking of the *spaces of our intimacy, the centres of (our) fate*; he is speaking of our memories, those powers that, *securely fixed in space*, remain coiled within us ready to spring and inform our lives with immediacy and our thoughts with urgency.

In his *Poetics of Space* Bachelard writes:

We have the impression that by staying in the motionlessness of its shell, the creature is preparing temporal explosions, not to say whirlwinds of being.

And in *The Poetics of Revery*:

*The passionate being prepares his explosions and his exploits in …
solitude.*

The shell, the yellow tiger, the crowing cock, the moon — these are the potencies in which time is compressed in the form of memories. To write is to engage a waking dream, to, in solitude, prepare a whirlwind. Says Bachelard:

… daydreams illuminate the synthesis of immemorial and recollected. In this remote region, memory and imagination remain associated, each one working for their mutual deepening.

For Bachelard, Time has but one reality — that of the instant. The instant is our solitude stripped bare, stripped down to its essential potencies — its Deep Zoo.

◆

The shapes of time are the prey we want to capture.
— George Kubler, *The Shape of Time*

When I was a child, I came upon the dead body of a red fox in the woods; it was early summer and the fox's belly was burning brightly with yellow bees. A species of animate calligraphy, the bees rose and fell in a swarm that revealed, then concealed, the corpse. Yellow and black they tigered it and they glamorized it, too — transforming what otherwise might have seemed horrible into a thing of rare beauty. It is no accident that my first novel opens with the death of a creature in a wood.

If I have, throughout this essay, dwelled on the potencies of what I've been calling the Deep Zoo, it is because it is the work of the writer to move beyond the simple definitions or descriptions of things — which is of limited interest after all — and to bring a dream to life through the alchemy of language; to move from the street — the place of received ideas — into the forest — the place of the unknown.

But the Deep Zoo's attraction is not sufficient. We must take care that our books do not resemble those 17th century wonder-rooms or 19th century parlours with their meaningless jumbles of stuffed bears, kayaks, giant lobsters and assorted stools. In other words, just as the museum of Natural History has contributed to, perhaps *enabled* our practical knowledge of the phenomenal world — and do not forget that the development of the museum coincides with the exclusion of Christian orthodoxy from the process of scientific inquiry — so must the books we write be free of those restraints that impede aesthetic invention; so must they be *enabled* by the rigours of intellectual coherence. Again, if we are to be quickened by the prime qualities of the Deep Zoo, we cannot, nevertheless, allow our books to be determined by excess or arbitrariness. Ideas and language deserve our chronic, our acute attention. After all, a book is above all a place to think, and the lightness of thoughtfulness our way of approaching the truth.

It is our capacity for moral understanding that enables us to interpret the world and to act thoughtfully and with autonomy. As psychoanalysis demonstrates, knowledge of ourselves and the world allows us to heal, to transcend the moral darkness that suffocates and blinds us. The process of writing a book is similar as it reveals to the writer what is hidden within her: writing is a reading of the self and of the world. *It is a process of knowledge.* That is why the lost roads and uncharted territories of the world's maze deserve our interest. If a book is a place to think, it is a pragmatic place, a place of experiment and discovery, a *battleground* (Calvino's word) where the orthodoxies — religious, political, neurotic — that interfere with clairvoyance, are dismantled and replaced by a new order. In other words, to write in the light of childhood's burning alcohol, with the irresistible ink of tigers and the cautious uncaging of our own Deep Zoo, we need to be attentive and fearless — above all very curious — and all at the same time.

In Maria Dermout's *The Ten Thousand Things*, a living sea snail in a box guards memories in the shapes of small, disparate objects. When the snail dies it is replaced — a spiritual manipulation that is also an act of magic. Resurgent, the memories continue to inform the world with a playful, essential and erotic mystery. Writes Borges:

In my soul the afternoon grows wider and I reflect.

— *Dream Tigers*

BIBLIOGRAPHY

Gaston Bachelard, *The Poetics of Space*, Beacon Press, Boston, 1969.
_____, *The Poetics of Revery*, Beacon Press, Boston, 1969.

Jorge Luis Borges, *Labyrinths*, Modern Library, New York, 1983.
_____, *Dream Tigers*, University of Texas Press, 1989.
_____, *Seven Nights*, New Directions, New York, 1984.

Italo Calvino, *Six Memos for the Next Millennium*, Harvard University Press, Cambridge, 1988.
_____, *Cosmicomics*, Harcourt Brace, Orlando, 1968.

Maria Dermout, *The Ten Thousand Things*, Simon and Schuster, 1958.

Johan Huizinga, *Homo Ludens*, Beacon Press, Boston, 1955.

Immanuel Kant, *Grounding for the Metaphysics of Morals*, translated by James W. Ellington, Hackett Publishing Company, Indianapolis, 1993.

George Kubler, *The Shape of Time*, Yale University Press, 1962.

Giovanni Mariotti, *Le Bestiaire d'Aloys Zötl*, F. M. Ricci, Paris, 1979.

Ovid, *The Metamorphoses*, Penguin, Middlesex, 1986.

Marquis de Sade, *The 120 Days of Sodom and Other Writings*, compiled and translated by Austryn Wainhouse and Richard Seaver, Grove Press, New York, 1966.

——, *Juliette*, translated by Austryn Wainhouse, Grove Press, New York, 1988.

F.M.R. no.1. Edited by Franco Maria Ricci. Franco Maria Ricci, New
York, 1984.

Dreaming Paradise, Martial and Snoeck, Rotterdam, 1996.

www.ingramcontent.com/pod-product-compliance
Lightning Source LLC
Chambersburg PA
CBHW031003090426
42737CB00008B/654